The Walking Bus

By Annette Smith

Illustrations by Naomi C. Lewis

Emma and Matthew went out to the car at 8 o'clock.

3

4

Mum came outside
to look at the car.

Mum shut the door.

Today we will go to school in a walking bus.

Matthew looked at Emma.

Mum is playing a trick on us.

On the way,
they saw Jimmy.

Jimmy!
This is a walking bus.

12

Come on Jimmy!

It's fun to walk to school.

Jimmy went with them.

Let's come to school in our walking bus tomorrow, too.